The Quest for Contentment

To Tami

Thanks for your support and enjoy! Contentment is a learned behavior.

Dr. Martin Freeman

MARTIN FREEMAN

ISBN 978-1-0980-6903-2 (paperback)
ISBN 978-1-0980-6904-9 (digital)

Copyright © 2021 by Martin Freeman

All rights reserved. No part of this publication may be reproduced, distributed, or transmitted in any form or by any means, including photocopying, recording, or other electronic or mechanical methods without the prior written permission of the publisher. For permission requests, solicit the publisher via the address below.

Christian Faith Publishing, Inc.
832 Park Avenue
Meadville, PA 16335
www.christianfaithpublishing.com

Printed in the United States of America

Dr. Martin Freeman has taken the words and concepts of the Apostle Paul in Philippians Chapter four, and given them a fresh voice for this moment. Contentment is not a fruit of the Spirit, but it is a gift from that Spirit when one surrenders their life to Christ. Dr. Freeman demonstrates that contentment comes when you trust God with every situation and view all of your circumstances through the lenses of faith. Contentment is that one pursuit that when you discover it and it possesses you, you will never let it go. Dr. Freeman's insights have obviously been invaluable to him during his life's journey. I believe these insights that have blessed his life, will bless all of ours.

—Dr. C. Jay Matthews I, Pastor,
Mount Sinai-Friendship United

The past year 2020 tells us that we must have new spiritual voices to clearly and powerfully transport ancient spiritual wisdom to our modern dilemmas. Dr. Freeman's book "The Quest for Contentment" is that new voice. Contentment is revolutionary in the same way that nonviolent resistance to injustice is revolutionary. Contentment is an antidote for the many dangerous psychological dis(eases) humans are experiencing. Dr. Freeman's book shows us how to prioritize and practice this wisdom.

—Dr. Homer Warren, Retired Professor,
Youngstown State University

Dr. Martin Freeman, a prolific twenty-first century biblical erudite continuing in the prophetic tradition of speaking truth to power, approaches these times and the current fears, frustrations, and foolishness with Holy Spirit guided insights in this his first book, and sure to be an instant classic. Martin, in this work, challenges and encourages each reader to exchange their horizontal outlook in order to gain heavenly perspective, walk in divine promise, and experience the power of God via the secret weapon, contentment! I am sure that as you read and apply the principles discussed in this work, and as written in the Holy Scriptures, you too will be able to experience contentment and peace in the midst of the storm, and "do all things through Christ who give you strength!" (Philippians 4:13 NIV)

—Garrick Matlock, Pastor,
Restoration Life Ministries

Contents

Preface 7

Introduction 11

1 Contentment—Let's Get an Understanding 13

2 The Origin of Contentment 17

3 Contentment: A Learned Behavior 20

4 Contentment = Delighting in the Lord 31

5 Consequences of Discontentment 36

6 Conquering Materialism 43

7 Money, Money, Money 50

8 Cultivating Contentment 56

9 Characteristics of Contentment 61

Conclusion 67

PREFACE

The purpose for writing this book originates out of watching man attempt to navigate a pandemic called Coronavirus that appears to have apprehended the world causing medical, social, financial, and economic disruption. As a result of the virus, man was asked to engage in social distancing and to shelter in place.

During this tumultuous time of affliction, I became weary, worried, and worn. I was restless, lacking the inward, gracious, quiet spirit that joyfully rests in God's providence (contentment). As often said at professional football games when plays are under review, "Upon further review," I was discontent.

As a result of my discontented spirit, I began to pray that God would teach me how to recognize how he upholds, governs, and sustains all things by his infinite power (1 Chron. 29:11–12; Psalm 24:1, 115:3, 135:6). This is when God's providence manifest itself.

After careful examination of Scripture, I realized that to be content is inextricably linked to God's providence. In other words, resting in God's providence is the bridge to my pursuit of contentment. A heart that is inwardly, graciously, and quiet rests in God's power.

I'm thankful for the hymn of Horatio Spafford that provides a spiritual equilibrium necessary to eradicate my discontentment. In the hymn "It Is Well," he writes:[1]

> *When peace like a river, attendeth my way,*
> *When sorrows like sea billows roll;*

---

[1] Horatio Spafford, "It Is Well," 1873

Whatever my lot, Thou hast taught me to know
It is well, it is well, with my soul.

Refrain
It is well, (it is well),
With my soul, (with my soul)
It is well, it is well, with my soul.

Though Satan should buffet, though trials should come,
Let this blest assurance control,
That Christ has regarded my helpless estate,
And hath shed his own blood for my soul.

My sin, oh, the bliss of this glorious thought!
My sin, not in part but the whole,
Is nailed to the cross, and I bear it no more,
Praise the Lord, praise the Lord, O my soul!

For me, be it Christ, be it Christ hence to live:
If Jordan above me shall roll,
No pang shall be mine, for in death as in life,
Thou wilt whisper Thy peace to my soul.
But Lord, 'tis for Thee, for Thy coming we wait,
The sky, not the grave, is our goal;
Oh, trump of the angel! Oh, voice of the Lord!
Blessed hope, blessed rest of my soul.

And Lord, haste the day when the faith shall be sight,
The clouds be rolled back as a scroll;
The trump shall resound, and the Lord shall descend,
A song in the night, oh my soul!

    This song is refreshing in that it clearly conveys the reason why God calls his children to be content regardless of anything and everything they may be going through, have gone through, and will go through in this life.

THE QUEST FOR CONTENTMENT

As I opened my Bible to study, brooding over various passages of Scripture, I was reminded of how pure, and life changing our walk in Christ can be when we accept the truth that God's Word is perfect (Psalm 19:7–14).

Over the course of many weeks, I began to ask and seek direction on how to align myself with identifying, understanding, and living a life of contentment. God began to show me what contentment is, where it originates and how to sustain it. I put pen to paper, talked with pastors, and worked to exhaustion on how to know what contentment is, how to grasp it and practically apply it to life.

I'm thankful for the time God gave me to discover the position, perspective, and power that contentment yields when I acquiesce to his grace extended to me. God enrolled me into the school of contentment to discover that I must learn and apply what I was writing before I could disseminate the findings to others.

The quest for contentment must not be a transient sprint but a far-reaching journey into the deep truths of God's Word. The journey is ongoing, requiring a mind released from the entrapments of the world (Colossians 3:1–3), a heart longing for his refreshing (Psalm 37:3–4), and a soul that says yes to his will (Psalm 62:1,5).

I'm grateful for the many voices, listening ears and hands that brought comfort and succor to this project. Thank you all at Christian Faith Publishing for your guidance and service in publishing books that fuel the world.

Thank you, Dr. Homer Warren, for your producer consciousness view, related to contentment. Your intellectual acumen is quiet but far reaching.

Thank you, Pastor Garrick Matlock, my brother, friend, and fellow pastor for your prolific biblical insight, discussions, and guidance on contentment.

Thank you to my family, for your continued inspiration to pursue this lofty goal of writing a book to help others in their quest for contentment.

Thank you to my God, for your grace and mercy. You have allowed me to move through this continuum to do that which I've longed for. To complete this project has been life changing but I realize the importance because, *"All scripture is given by inspiration of God, and is profitable for doctrine, for reroof, for correction, for instruction in righteousness: That the man of God may be perfect, thoroughly furnished unto all good works" (2 Timothy 3:1–17).*

Introduction

Are you satisfied with your life? Is there a prevailing peace enveloping you? Does the Spirit of God control you? Can you say that the link between contentment and providence in your life is God's grace?

If you are not satisfied with things in your life, it is likely your human desires are getting in the way of God's desires. When you desire what he desires, you will experience contentment to the fullest.

I would be dishonest from the onset to communicate that I've lived or have been living in a state of contentment. The word contentment is a word that has eluded me, though I've tried to grasp it throughout my Christian life. My quest to live a life of contentment comes with baggage just as many in search of contentment. Within the course of this book I hope to define contentment, how to biblically pursue contentment, and ultimately sustain a life of contentment.

I'm mindful of a man named Job who in The Old Testament learned and practiced this secret of contentment. Job lost everything including his home, his wealth, his family, even his health but was able to say, *"Naked I came from my mother's womb, and naked I will depart. The Lord gave and the Lord has taken away; may the name of the Lord be praised" (Job 1:21).* Job, during the catastrophic events of his life, practiced contentment and continued to believe in God.

Is contentment a fleeting idea or a biblical principle God strategically placed in Scripture for man to learn? Has contentment become an ancient practice superseded by the post-modern church? Has the church lost its efficacy, direction, and intent to practice contentment?

Paul teaches us otherwise, *"Not that I speak in respect of want; for I have learned, in whatsoever state I am, therewith to be content"*

(Philippians 4:11). Paul is teaching us that contentment must be learned and that it isn't a displaced spiritual discipline. Contentment must be prioritized and practiced.

I pray, moving forward, that you will not be discouraged when working toward contentment. You can learn as did Paul that contentment is attainable, that God commands and enables you by his grace to experience this inward, gracious, quiet spirit as you rest in the joy of his providence.

1

Contentment—Let's Get an Understanding

Contentment is the only real wealth.
—*Alfred Nobel*

Verta Mae Freeman, with her actions in time of uncertainty, gave me a clear example of contentment. I'm forever grateful for her example. I'm still indebted to the model of biblical contentment she exhibited. My mother personified what Jeremiah Burroughs biblically defined as contentment: *"Christian contentment is that sweet, inward, quiet, gracious frame of spirit, which freely submits to and delights in God's wise and fatherly disposal in every condition."*[2]

Mother, during a trip to the ER, was told by the doctor that there was probable cause for cancer regarding a biopsy taken of her lungs. Mother immediately seemed to exude a quiet spirit saying, *"Whatever the results I've lived well past my expectations and I'm thankful."* What propelled her to not complain but give thanks? My mother also recognized the power of providence. What does providence mean? It refers to God's work in which he upholds, governs, and sustains all things by his infinite power. My mother realized that it was God that kept her and if she should live it would be him who would continue to keep her.

---

[2] Especially Jeremiah Burroughs, The Rare Jewel of Christian Contentment (Edinburgh: Banner of Truth, 1979) p. 3

It was on a cool day in October of 2018 that upon arriving at the doctor's office to review the results of the test that I braced myself for the results that would be the defining moment in my relationship with my mom. It was on that day she taught me the power of contentment. The doctor gave his diagnosis, prognosis, and needed prescription. It was cancer. Chemotherapy was the recommended treatment.

Quiet swept the room until my mother, in response to the needed prescription (chemotherapy) communicated, *"I will not take chemotherapy. I want to enjoy whatever time I have with my children, grandchildren, and family."* The strength she exhibited could only be realized because of God's grace that links contentment and providence.

There are people who've found themselves in a same predicament, but contentment eluded them. Their cry was "Why me? I don't deserve this lot. I need more time." I pray that in times of difficulty you will learn contentment as did Paul.

I'm mindful that the opposite of contentment is discontentment. Discontentment comes when we are restless, unhappy, unsatisfied, curious. A discontent spirit is the result of our quest for the flashy, shiny things in life. A bigger home, more money, and greater success is often the cause for discontent. Not that I'm against the niceties mentioned; however, the Christian must seek God first (Matthew 6:25–33).

Contrast this with the heart of the apostle Paul who said, *"Not that I speak in respect of want; for I have learned, in whatsoever state I am, therewith to be content" (Phil. 4:11).* Paul is letting us know that life is not about more or less but what we need. Contentment is being described by Paul as a satisfaction with the goodness of God, knowing he knows what we need and what is best for us.

In my writing this book I came across a Proverb that says, *"A contented mind is a perpetual feast."* It speaks further to how contentment can impact each of us differently. For example, Kahlil Gibran, a Lebanese-American writer, poet, and visual artist, wrote, *"Once, when my feet were bare, and I had not the means of obtaining shoes, I came to the chief of Kufah in a state of much dejection, and saw there a man who had no feet. I returned thanks to God and acknowledged his mercies and endured my want of shoes with patience."*[3]

The Coronavirus quickened me to learn true contentment and as I sat *"sheltering in place."* This virus is teaching me to accept the lot I've been given, and to exhibit a thankful attitude about life. The world is caught in the cross-hare of a decline in our global economy, incapacitated health care system, and fear. Contentment should relieve us of the fear, uncertainty, anxiety, and doubt because Isaiah said, *"Thou wilt keep him in perfect peace, whose mind is stayed on thee: because he trusteth in thee"* (Isa. 26:3).

The world we live in has become materialistic to a degree never seen in human history. When we look out over the landscape of humanity all signs point to a world of people who have become *"shopaholics"* and sharks in a feeding frenzy! Many people are overwhelmed in debt to the degree that bankruptcy seems to be their only solution. "Easy credit" continues to appeal to the unwary and the "buy now and pay later" craze continues. The fish have taken the bait and are running with it, but when the devil sets the hook and plunges the world into a monetary crisis of unprecedented proportions, most of them will be reeled in and on his dinner table.

True contentment is mirrored in the life of Jacob's son, Joseph (Genesis, chapters 37–50). It would do the readers of this book well to read and discover that the life of Joseph was one of contentment. Through no fault of his own, he was subjected to numerous setbacks that would have destroyed lesser men. But he did not compromise and through it all remained faithful to God even though he was falsely accused and imprisoned for years. Then, in due time, God used him to deliver and protect the very brothers who had betrayed him—thereby miraculously preserving the nation of Israel, through which the Messiah was to come. So even amid trials and tribulations, Joseph exhibited godly contentment and continued to walk by faith.

I purport to you that there is a danger in misinterpreting this often misunderstood word. If contentment is to be learned and prac-

---

[3] The Gulistan by Sa'di, Chapter III, Story 19

ticed, then we must grasp its meaning and dispel what it is not. As we move forward together, I trust the inward working of God's spirit will move you to allow his grace to set you at peace so that contentment will become your way of life.

2

The Origin of Contentment

Contentment, then, is the product of a heart resting in God. It is the soul's enjoyment of that peace that passes all understanding. It is the outcome of my will being brought into subjection to the divine will. It is the blessed assurance that God does all things well, and is, even now, making all things work together for my ultimate good.
—*Arthur W. Pink*

The primary way to experience contentment is learning it's origin, why it's difficult to achieve, and how to attain it. God has provided man with the roadmap that allows him to navigate safely to the determined destination, that being heaven.

The ultimate theme of the Bible is God's relationship with man. God has worked through history to restore the broken relationship between Himself and his people. One of the many virtues available to man, because of being in relationship with God, is contentment. Understanding God to be at the center of contentment is pivotal because he is contentment. The Bible paints a kaleidoscopic picture of God as both the object and model of contentment.

The Origin

Mike Bennett shares, "Man has, throughout human history, searched for contentment. Finding contentment and satisfaction has been difficult, even painstaking for some. This quest has led man to all the wrong places and when thinking contentment has been found he discovers it was fleeting and temporary."[4] For example, it is common and seems logical to conclude that if everyone were prosperous, everyone would automatically be content and satisfied.

The Psalmist declares, *"Surely I have behaved and quieted myself, as a child that is weaned of his mother: my soul is even as a weaned child" (Psalm 131:2)*. As children of God we must depend upon God's providence for the way and time of bringing us into relationship and total dependence on him. Further, the child of God must entertain humility, not aiming at lofty things, but modeling as little children in innocence and simplicity.

Is physical abundance the cause of contentment? What is the real source of deep, lasting contentment and eternal satisfaction? We'll see it's not prosperity that will bring contentment. It's something much more important. It begins and ends with God.

Solomon concludes in the book of Ecclesiastes that contentment is rooted in God: *"Fear God and keep his commandments, for this is man's all" (Ecclesiastes 12:13)*. God is at the center of all contentment. Solomon goes on to further explain that, *"The fear of the Lord leads to life, and he who has it will abide in satisfaction; he will not be visited with evil" (Prov. 19:23)*. When we put God first, fearing to displease and disappointment him, then we are on the road to experiencing contentment.

Difficulty achieving contentment
Let's look together to the book of Ecclesiastes to unlock the truth on why it is difficult to achieve contentment. There are verses in the biblical book of Ecclesiastes that tell us of the origin of as well as why it's challenging to achieve contentment: *"The eye is not satisfied with seeing, nor the ear filled with hearing" (1:8)*. "All the labor of man is for his mouth, and yet the soul is not satisfied" *(6:7)*. Regardless

---

[4] Mike Bennett, What's the Real Source of Contentment? Life, Hope & Truth

of what we see, hear or taste our experiences will be temporary. Man will always find it difficult to achieve contentment because of his ego-centric proclivity and narcissism. Solomon wants us to know that the eye and ear represent all the human faculties, which are constantly occupied with the pursuit of good, but without being satisfied. Man continues in his vain pursuit to find contentment in the things of the world but soon grows weary.

Attaining it

Man's heart remains wicked now just as in times past (Jeremiah 17:9). Man's desires, pursuits, and complaints have not changed but God is still the same (Hebrews 13:8). Let us not expect contentment in the creature but heed the call of the Psalmist, *"Trust in the Lord, and do good; so shalt thou dwell in the land and verily thou shalt be fed. Delight thyself also in the Lord: and he shall give thee the desires of thine heart"* (Psalm 37:3–4).

I urge you to delight yourself in the word, will, and way of God so that your access to contentment is realized. Purposing in your heart not to covet earthly possessions, enjoyments, and distinctions qualifies you for the best God has to offer. The Gospel of Matthew gives us insight and direction, *"But seek ye first the kingdom of God, and his righteousness; and all these things shall be added unto you"* (Matthew 6:33).

What is the object of your search predicated on? It is imperative that the search leads you to the reign of Christ and his kingdom. This means avoiding delight in the search for worldly objects as they are temporal. God calls his people to set our desires and efforts after heavenly things (Matthew 6:20).

3

Contentment: A Learned Behavior

We often think contentment is something that happens to us, rather than something that we take pains to learn.
—*Nancy Wilson*

John W. Kimball gives a simple definition of learned behavior this way: *"A learned behavior is one that an organism develops as a result of experience."*[5]

Dan Nosowitz provides an illustration saying, *"If you own a dog or have a friend who owns a dog you probably know that dogs can be trained to do things like sit, beg, roll over, and play dead. These are examples of learned behaviors and dogs can be capable of significant learning."*[6]

In no way have I considered dogs to be superior to man; however, the example drives the point home that contentment can be learned. I believe our desire to know, to understand, to grow, to communicate, to transform increases the value of the learning experience.

In this chapter I hope to inspire you to develop the attitude of Paul who teaches us that contentment is a way of life, that we must never stop aspiring toward a quest to attain it. Contentment must be learned and practiced.

---

[5] Kimball, John W. "Some Simple Forms of Learned Behavior." Kimball's Biology Pages, Last modified February 17, 2011
[6] Dan Nosowitz, "I Met the World's Smartest Dog," Popular Science, last modified August 26, 2013

THE QUEST FOR CONTENTMENT

It's time we come front and center with the classic passage on contentment being a learned behavior. Listen to the testimony of a man who often found himself in various circumstances and situations, which clearly delineates that this great virtue can be learned:

> *But I rejoiced in the Lord greatly, that now at the last your care of me hath flourished again; where in ye were also careful, but ye lacked opportunity. Not that I speak in respect of want; for I have learned, in whatsoever state I am, therewith to be content. I know both how to be abased, and I know how to abound: everywhere and in all things I am instructed both to be full and to be hungry, both to abound and to suffer need. I can do all things through Christ which strengtheneth me. (Philippians 4:10–13)*

Paul declares that every good gift is by the immediate providence of God, then proceeds to acknowledge God's people who for a season were not able to supply his basic needs. His communication is not of complaint because of want because he expresses his appreciation for what the church provided (Phil. 4:14).

Understanding the Word
Paul quickly begins his ascent toward how he attained contentment, *"For I have learned" (Phil. 4:11).* The "I" in the Greek language is emphatic because it speaks to the discontent he experienced apart from God (Phil. 3:7–12). He now speaks as a man empowered by the Holy Spirit (Jn. 14:26), and God's teachings (Rom. 5:8).

The use of the word "content," in verse 11, is commonly translated to mean *"self-sufficient."* William B. Barclay concludes, *"The Greek philosophers described contentment to be one of the chief virtues and was frequently described as non-attachment or not being dependent on others."*[7] Let's be clear, this is not what Paul is describing here in verse 11, that in fact he's communicating that self-sufficiency is attained via God's unmerited favor.

We must not arrogate ourselves to have any power to enlighten our minds or change the once wickedness of our hearts but, remain luminous to being mere vessels of clay in the hands of God. Man's ability to think, create, and act of doing is result of God not our own sufficiency (2 Cor. 3:5).

Paul's context of *"self-sufficiency,"* is not contingent upon outward experiences but the inward quietness that comes from God when accepting our lot regardless of where we are or what situation we encounter. The type of contentment Paul describes in Philippians 4 drives home God's self-sufficiency. God, being identified and defined as self-sufficient, means he possesses within himself every quality, ability, and supernatural command with never-ending measure. Every attribute or mighty and wonderful power is his endlessly. God wants for nothing and lacks nothing; he is complete.

Bible scholars speak to self-sufficiency as a characteristic. It is, without question, God is independent. God does not need anyone or anything. God is self-sufficient (Col. 1:15–20). Knowing God is at the center of understanding how to be content. This truth drove Paul to learn contentment.

The Beauty of Learned Contentment
Author F.B. Meyer wrote,

> *If we would find contentment, let us go to homes where women are crippled with rheumatism, or dying of cancer, where comforts are few, where long hours of loneliness are not broken by the intrusion*

---

[7] William B. Barclay, *The Secret of Contentment* (P & R Publishing, 2010), p. 31

of friendly faces, where the pittance of public charity hardly suffices for necessary need, to say nothing of comfort, it is there that contentment reveals itself like a shy flower. How often in the homes of the wealthy one has missed it, to find it in the homes of the poor! How often it is wanting where health is buoyant, to be discovered where disease is wearing out the strength! So it was with the Apostle, who was in the saddest part of his career. Bound to the Roman soldier, enclosed in some narrow apartment, in touch with only a few friends who made an effort to discover him, away from the happy scenes of earlier years, and anticipating Nero's bar, he breaks out into these glorious expressions of equanimity. He had learned how to be abased in the valley of the shadow; he wore the flower heartsease in his buttonhole.[8]

What is your quest? Is it for what is better? What is next? Man is never satisfied because he wants better employment with a salary commensurate to his education and experience. We desire a better golf swing, a better body, fastest car. Man is in a constant quest for the next thing, next phenomenal purchase, the best education. Why are we never satisfied, never content, and envious of those who have what we have not attained or accumulated?

How could Paul make such an audacious statement in Philippians 4:11? Paul had a relationship rooted and grounded in God, that his contentment was not about what he possessed but who possessed him (Gal. 2:20). When man looks horizontally at what others possess, he will always dwell in discontent. When man looks vertically with a focus on God recognizing he is his source, substance, and provider then contentment will be his (Phil. 4:19).

---

[8] *The Epistle to the Philippians,* F. B. Meyer

Nature of Being Content

Much has been discussed, discovered, and developed as it relates to contentment. As we turn our attention forward, how can we learn the nature of being content? Paul gives us clear insight on how he learned contentment and how we can begin to learn this virtue.

Paul testifies that he's learned to be content; therefore, this virtue can be attained. Paul didn't achieve contentment because he was an apostle, could speak many languages, or because of his heritage. Paul realized he was strengthened by God (Phil. 4:13). Let's be clear that this passage doesn't give us green light to believe that God gives us the power to do whatever we want but he wants us to acquire this virtue for growth in holiness.

The enemy of holiness is sin which causes a discontented heart. In order to progress toward holiness, sin must be eradicated which God's transforming power is able to be done in us. "But we all, with open face beholding as in a glass the glory of the Lord, are changed into the same image from glory to glory, even as by the Spirit of the Lord" (2 Cor. 3:18). The sanctifying work of the Holy Spirit allows us to pursue contentment and this is how Paul was able to attain this virtue.

What is this great passage in Philippians teaching us? Does contentment come naturally? Is there a mystery to contentment? Let's look at the nature of contentment:

Contentment is a learned state (behavior).

We are living in a period of time that finds our hearts and minds bombarded with outside stimuli contrary to God's will for our lives. We are asked to learn many things, sometimes to our detriment (2 Tim. 3:7). We must learn to focus our learning toward that which will empower us to live fulfilled lives in Christ, but the challenge becomes recognizing that Christian contentment and the pursuit of it are at odds with the thinking of this age. Oliver B. Green shares,

THE QUEST FOR CONTENTMENT

"Certainly if believers understand the "old man" as opposed to the new, there would be much less backsliding than is in evidence today."[9]

Barclay says, *"Christian satisfaction and contentment come primarily through our relationship with God in Christ."*[10] The Christian must have an attitude of work to attain contentment. It must be learned, studied, and brooded over. We must condition ourselves to rethink how we think to achieve this elusive virtue (Phil. 4:8). God's way is the only way to achieve contentment and any other way is a recipe for failure.

Paul learned contentment through bad situations and circumstances. He trusted God and realized that, "Godliness with contentment is great gain" (1 Tim. 6:6). Paul learned that godly contentment is not dependent upon circumstances or suffering. Remember, *"For what glory is it, if when ye be buffeted for your faults, ye shall take it patiently? But if, when ye do well, and suffer for it, ye take it patiently, this is acceptable with God"* (1 Pet. 2:20).

Contentment is accepting what we have.

America, at the time of this writing, is experiencing a virus (Coronavirus/Covid19) that is ravaging the world. How does a believer find contentment in a world that's under so much duress? We must not find contentment but learn it and know that it starts with Jesus Christ. Paul reminds us that, *"For we brought nothing into this world, and it is certain we can carry nothing out, and having food and raiment let us be therewith content"* (1 Tim. 6:7–8).

Are you comfortable with what you possess? Is your home a place of peace? Is money driving you? Paul is trying to help those who are consumed by possessions and circumstances. Why? Listen, *"But they that will be rich fall into temptations and snare, and into*

---

[9] Oliver B. Green, *The Two Natures* (The Gospel Hour, Inc.)
[10] William B. Barclay, *The Secret of Contentment* (P & R Publishing, 2010), p. 126

many foolish and hurtful lusts, which drown men in destruction and perdition" (1 Tim. 6:9).

Jacqueline Pearce says, *"Contentment means to be happy with what you have, who you are, and where you are. It is respecting the reality of the present. It is appreciating what you do have and where you are in life."*[11]

I purport to you that contentment isn't just a matter of being okay with your situation in life and never attempting to improve it. I believe it's a matter of being content with what you have yet aspiring as a human you will ever be trying to improve regardless of how happy you are. If this is not the case, you've given up on life.

As you aspire to accept what you have, do three things:

a. *Raise your awareness*—refresh your memory and be grateful for what you already have
b. *Welcome what you can't change*—stop forcing things to be the way you want them to be
c. *Practice patience*—let God unfold your life and order your steps

Contentment is not external but internal

Paul says he learned, *"Whatsoever state I am, therewith to be content" (Phil. 4:11).* A person who is content has learned that his inner state isn't determined by external circumstances. A person whose life is manifested from the inside out doesn't hang his happiness to his 401K plan, to his child being admitted to Harvard Law School, or to owning a Maserati. The content person realizes that regardless of his position, prestige, prominence, power, he will never be content apart

---

[11] Jacqueline Pearce, The Essence of Contentment: How Acceptance Promotes Happiness, September 11, 2019

from God. The content man, woman, boy, or girl has learned to look inwardly to gain contentment in life.

How was Paul able to separate his inward emotions from his outward emotions? Notice the word "learned." Paul understood that the ability to be content with what God had already provided didn't come naturally but was something he could learn.

Satan will continue to lie to us and use every means necessary to trip us up (1 Jn. 2:15–17). Satan will always tell us that as long as we don't have what we want we'll be unhappy. Satan continuously dangles the carrot of temptation before us. Believers must not fall into the trap of the enemy that leads to discontent. God wants believers to be content no matter what our external circumstances may be. We can learn from him to be content, *"And Jesus saith unto him, 'The foxes have holes, and the birds of the air have nests; but the Son of man hath not where to lay his head'"* (Matt. 8:20).

Contentment is accepting the will of God.
Paul again draws our attention to Philippians 4:12, *"I know both how to be abased, and I know how to abound: everywhere and in all things I am instructed both to be full and to be hungry, both to abound and to suffer need."*

God predestined Paul to experience many states to which he kept him through them all. He had experienced all things; want as well as plenty, hunger and food in abundance; every variety of condition.

Contentment is accepting from God's hand what he sends because we know that he is a good God and wants to care for his people. Accepting what God gives us is critical to his will and the learning curve moving believers to contentment. God will supply all of our needs and keep us in times of hardships, suffering, and pain.

If we fail to surrender to the will of God, we will forever be discontented. Our freedom will be suffocated. We will be in bondage to our desires. Our relationships will be poisoned with jealousy and competition. Potential blessings will be sacrificed. Discontentment has the potential to destroy our peace, rob us of joy, make us miserable, and tarnish our witness.

The Prescription for Contentment

Contentment is a different way of living; therefore, Paul spoke as he did in Philippians 4 because it is elusive. Contentment is not acquired because of age, attained by intelligence nor by wealth gained. Contentment is gained because of professing our faith in Christ. Contentment must be learned, *"I've learned to be content."*

Jeremiah Burroughs said this about contentment,

> *Contentment in every condition is a great art, a spiritual mystery. It is to be learned and to be learned as a mystery. And so Paul affirms, "I know both how to be abased, and I know how to abound: everywhere and in all things I am instructed." The word that is translated instructed is derived from the word that signifies "mystery." It is just as if he had said, "I have learned the mystery of this business." Contentment is to be learned as a great mystery.*[12]

Richard Swenson helpfully describes the prescription for learning contentment in this manner:[13]

Rx: 1 Learn through intentionality—We must be intentional as was Paul when he said, *"I press toward the mark for the prize of the high calling of God in Christ Jesus" (Phil. 3:14).*

Rx: 2 Learn through experiences—Paul learned that his life experiences were spiritual experiences (2 Cor. 11:23–28). Paul went to the

---
[12] Jeremiah Burroughs, The Rare Jewel of Christian Contentment (Edinburgh, Scotland: The Banner of Truth, 1648, 1987), p. 17–18
[13] Richard A. Swenson, MD Contentment: The Secret to a Lasting Calm, 79–98

same contentment school that we are going through. Paul practiced, grew in it, nurtured it, and learned it through his experiences.

Rx: 3 Learn by being in the presence of God—*Learning the secret of contentment comes from daily fellowship with and obedience to his will. Therefore, the Psalmist said, "Thou will shew me the path of life; in thy presence is fullness of joy; at thy right hand there are pleasures for evermore" (Psa. 16:11).*

Rx: 4 Learn through patient submission to Christ—*The biblical concept of submission is to place oneself under the authority of another. When we submit to God, we give our lives to his authority and control. We must choose to submit to God for the process of learning in order to grow spiritually. It is a process begun at salvation and ongoing with every choice that we make to submit ourselves to God. This process will continue until the Lord comes again or he calls us home. Let us submit to God just as his son submitted to him (Jn. 5:19, 6:38).*

Rx: 5 Learn by moderating our desires—*It is unusual to make large shifts in behavior, but if we are to learn contentment, we will need to challenge thinking and habits on a regular basis (Heb. 13:5).*

Rx: 6 Learn by adjusting our hearts—*The spiritual heart is the repository of our affections. This makes it a target-rich environment for a study of contentment. What is your heart set on? Let us follow Paul's admonition (Col. 3:1–2). David gives us greater admonition (Psa. 62:10). Jesus sums it up for us (Matt. 6:21).*

Rx: 7 Learn by daily choices—*We make choices daily. Our choices are so numerous we can't begin to name them all. Contentment is also a choice, and by making it frequently throughout the day, we train our wills to want what God wants for us. This is the process of becoming content.*

Rx: 8 Learn through patience—No wonder Paul had learned such contentment. Listen to his own words about how he learned patience (2 Cor. 11:23–28).

Rx: 9 Cultivate inner contentment—Paul acquired an internal fountain of sufficiency from God (Phil. 4:12). Let us be mindful that our homes, cars, money are wonderful; however, not the end. What really counts concerns our inner life and the source of our connection (Jn. 15:5).

Rx: 10 Don't look back—It is easy to become trapped in unpleasant destructive memories. Don't allow the circumstances of your past failures to handcuff you, stripping you of potential dreams (Phil. 3:13).

Rx: 11 Place our relationship with Christ above our relationship with things—The things of the world come and then they go. Move beyond the temporal and focus on the eternal (2 Cor. 4:18).

Rx. 12 Accept God's providence over our preference—Contentment is our glad submission wrapped in God's providence. Providence is God's perfect plan, and nothing can thwart his plan. The believer can either accept it or kick against it, but regardless, the plan of God will go forward. Paul knew this concept all too well (Acts 16:12–35). Thank God for his providence!

4

Contentment = Delighting in the Lord

*Do not spoil what you have by desiring what you have not;
remember that what you now have was once
among the things you only hoped for.*

—*Epicurus*

As I was spending quiet time, brooding over this theme of contentment, a thought captivated my mind. I asked the question, is there anything I'm discontent about? Reflection transported me down an avenue that eventually led to conviction and I confessed that what I was desiring disquieted my spirit. I was not resting in God's providence.

Although, the words content and delight are different there's a similarity to both. As has been discussed, being content is having an inward, gracious, quiet spirit that rests in God's providence. Delight is a word meaning, *"A high degree of pleasure, or satisfaction of mind; joy."*[14]

Similar but Not the Same

Let's work toward delineating the similarities and characteristics between those who are content and those who are not? Do they have anything in common? Is there a pattern?

---

[14] Merriam-Webster Dictionary

Rachael Carmon astutely observed, *"Contentment grows in proportion to trust. The more you trust God, the more content you become. The less you trust Him, the more discontent you are."*[15]

I ask if you believe that statement. Do you believe it, or have we settled, mistakenly accepting contentedness to be a byproduct of attainment, commercial success, or opportunity? Are you shocked that when an individual of wealth is so discontent that they could commit suicide? On the other hand, we are inspirited when we read of someone who has no positive financial means, who was known only to family and friends but so content in life that they positively impacted others?

Is there a formula to achieve contentment? Are there required steps to take? What if you were informed that contentment is nothing that can be achieved? I take the position that contentment is the output of mature faith and deep trust in God. In other words, contentment has nothing to do with externals and everything to do with accepting and responding to God's providence.

Contentment Is Trusting and Delighting in God

Over the years I've read Psalms 37 many times, more so, verses 3–4. *"Trust in the Lord and do good; so shalt thou dwell in the land, and verily thou shalt be fed. Delight thyself also in the Lord: and he shall give thee the desires of thine heart."* I've heard these verses quoted by Christians, preached over the pulpit, and talked about but most times not exegetically. Let's look at trusting God which is how we get to delighting in him.

As the believer seeks God (Matthew 6:33), contentment grows in proportion to his or her trust. Our trust is contingent upon the depth of our understanding and application of his Word, which in turn moves us toward contentment. The less you trust him, the more discontent you are. Put another way, *"your level of discontent betrays your mistrust of the Lord."*[16]

---
[15] Rachael Carmon, Contentment: A Measure of Trust, Living Before the Throne
[16] Adam Clarke Commentary, Psalm 37:5

THE QUEST FOR CONTENTMENT

How content one is directly influences their confidence in the sovereign God, that we can trust him. God can do what he declares, and he cannot lie (Romans 11:29). The immutability of the divine counsel is the safety of the saints. Every promise is yes and amen in Christ Jesus, and not one single word of the Lord shall ever fall to the ground. Why would man not trust and be content in God whose character, will, and covenant promises will never change!

Let us now turn our attention to how we are to delight ourselves in the Lord. Sometimes these churchy sayings get so overused that we aren't even sure what they mean anymore. *"Delight yourself in the Lord"* is one of those but allow me to work toward a biblical explanation.

To delight, not in earthly possessions, enjoyments, and distinctions, but in God, in knowing, loving, and worshipping him, and enjoying his love; and to delight in contemplation, devotion, and admiring praise, is to be spiritually-minded. Delighting in God is like an inhabitant having reached the celestial shores of heaven, and now qualifying for their delight.

Man, who embraces God's Word, knows he that seeks delight in worldly objects very seldom obtains the wishes of his heart but all the spiritual desires and requests that line up with delighting in his Word will be granted.

The secret to contentment that is driven by trust and delighting in God is knowing what God wants for you and wanting only what God wants. My prayer is that in learning to be content we trade in our fear for faith, our mistrust for confidence, and doubt for contentment. Trust God so that you can joyfully rest in the providence of God. Delight in God so that you are fulfilled and find peace on your journey.

This Davidic Psalm points the way to contentment. The Psalm provides four simple steps that will help the believer on the journey to contentment. You can have inner peace and contentment regardless of what others may do, if you will do these four things. God's formula is biblically proven.

Trust in the Lord

We must view trusting God through the lens of faith. Faith cures fretting, *"Trust in the Lord."* Faith has clearer optics which allow us to behold things as they really are so that we don't suffer from spiritual myopia. David encourages us further to know that true faith is actively obedient "and do good." Doing good is a fine remedy for fretting. There is a joy in holy activity which drives away the rust of discontent. he goes on to say, "so shalt thou dwell in the land." God doesn't want us wandering in the wilderness of murmuring but abiding in content and rest. David concludes with, "and verily thou shalt be fed." God will exercise his pastoral care over all his children. He will feed us his truth and the promise of God shall be a perpetual banquet (Psa. 37:25).

Delight in the Lord

What does it mean to *"delight"* in the Lord? It is to make the Lord the joy of your life. It is to develop a deep love relationship with him in which your only goal is to please him. The believer is commanded not to delight in earthly possessions, enjoyments, and distinctions, but in God. When the believer seeks to know, love, and worship God, all his spiritual desires and requests will be granted.

Commit Thy Way Unto the Lord

Bible scholar Adam Clarke says, *"The word "commit" provides us a visual used in ancient times of loading a camel. Whenever you loaded a camel, it would kneel down on its front legs so that you could roll the load it was to carry on to its back."*[17] Camels were the UPS of the ancient world. This is what we are to do—we are to roll our way on to the Lord of the covenant. You have a choice—you can attempt to carry your way yourself or you can roll it on the shoulders of our able Lord.

God implores the believer to roll the whole burden of life upon him. Place your cares, challenges, and conundrums with him. We are

---

[17] Ibid

to, *"Roll our burdens on to God as one who lays upon the shoulder of one stronger than himself that which he is not able to bear."*[18]

Rest in the Lord

Let us not discompose ourselves at what we see in this world. A fretful, discontented spirit is open to many temptations. The believer is not to complain at the direction (providence) of God, but silently and quietly acquiesce to his will, and delight in his judgments. We must learn to wait on the Lord without anger, envy and discontent.

---

[18] William De Burgh, D.D., in "A Commentary on the Book of Psalms." Dublin: 1860.

5

Consequences of Discontentment

When you are discontent, you always want more, more, more. Your desire can never be satisfied. But when you practice contentment, you can say to yourself, "Oh yes—I already have everything that I really need."
—*Dalai Lama*

How many of you reading believe that sin is at the core of discontentment, that Satan plants seeds of discontentment in our lives? If we are purveyors of truth, we'd admit we've been victims of watering the seeds of temptation that lead to discontent hearts. Discontentment is a toxicant that if not dealt with will take residence in your heart. It has a way of moving you to believe that all God has blessed you with is insufficient.

Discontentment can convince you that the home you're living in isn't as beautiful as someone else's on Facebook, so getting a bigger and better home is a must.

The power of a discontent heart can convince you that you need to buy that that new car, new set of golf clubs, new Michael Kors purse, knowing you're on a limited income but because you saw someone else with it, you feel it's right for you.

Discontentment can be so strong it will lead you away from a place or a season of life that God has pre-ordained for you, as a result you find yourself lured by the new and shiny that ultimately leaves you spiritually depleted.

Discontentment breeds the belief that God is keeping something from you that is better for you than what you have right now. The story of Eve in the garden is a classic convincing argument on how Satan uses people who are discontent:

> *Now the serpent was more subtle than any beast of the field which the Lord God had made. And he said unto the woman, Yea, hath God said, Ye shall not eat of every tree of the garden? And the woman said unto the serpent, We may eat of the fruit of the trees of the garden: But of the fruit of the tree which is in the midst of the garden, God hath said, Ye shall not eat of it, neither shall ye touch it, lest ye die. And the serpent said unto the woman, Ye shall not surely die: For God doth know that in the day ye eat thereof, then your eyes shall be opened, and ye shall be as gods, knowing good and evil. And when the woman saw that the tree was good for food, and that it was pleasant to the eyes, and a tree to be desired to make one wise, she took of the fruit thereof, and did eat, and gave also unto her husband with he; and he did eat.* (Gen. 3:1–6)

Cheyenne Olson shares, *"Discontentment is carbon monoxide to our soul."* She further communicates,

> *It's a silent killer that's odorless, tasteless, and invisible. It slips in unnoticed, robs us of joy and traps us in a prison of self-absorption and pride. It causes us to focus on what isn't instead of being grateful for the blessings that are.*[19]

---

[19] Cheyenne Olson, My 15 Minutes: Genesis 3:1, The Seeds of Discontentment

What caused Eve's discontentment with all that God had provided? Despite God's goodness, love, mercy, grace, and provision, Eve allowed the seed of doubt to grow and produce the fruit of sin. Listen to Satan's slick verbiage, *"Yea, hath God said"* (Gen. 3:1), as if God meant something different. Eve only needed to adhere to the command God gave,

> *And the Lord God took the man, and put him into the garden of Eden to dress it and to keep it. And the Lord God commanded the man, saying, "Of every tree of the garden thou mayest freely eat: But of the tree of the knowledge of good and evil, thou shalt not eat of it; for in the day that thou eatest thereof thou shalt surely die."* (Genesis 2:15–17)

Don Steward says,

> *Satan cast doubt on God's Word and character. He denied that God had Eve's best interest in mind. According to the serpent, God was holding something back from Adam and Eve that eating from the tree would provide them. The irony is that Adam and Eve were already like God in the sense they were created in his image.*[20]

Eve failed to heed God's command, thus prompting punishment meted out to Satan, Eve, and Adam (Gen. 3:14–24). It is evident that Eve didn't take heed of God's Word. The believer must know God's Word and make application of it. The believer must guard the heart (Prov. 4:23), from the temptations that manifest daily in our lives (1 Cor. 10:13).

---

[20] Don Stewart, Blue Letter Bible

I believe the church must do a better job of teaching as it relates to the craftiness of Satan who, as Cheyenne Olson says, knows are weaknesses:[21]

> He knows our weaknesses as well as our strengths.
> He knows our likes and dislikes.
> He knows what attracts us and what doesn't.
> He knows our wants, needs, and desires.
> He knows how to manipulate us.
> He knows which lure will be the most attractive, which will most likely snare us.

Cheyenne Olson implores believers that knowing the Scriptures and making practical application of his Word will sustain the believer in times of Satan's attacks:[22]

- To learn to be content with what you have (Phil. 3:11–13, Heb. 13:5).
- To give thanks in all circumstances (1 Thess. 5:18).
- To not give him an opportunity or a foothold (Eph. 4:27).
- To be wise to his schemes so we are not outwitted by him (2 Cor. 2:11).
- To know beyond a shadow of any doubt—*He* who is *in* us (Jesus) is greater than he (Satan) who is in the world (1 John 4:4).
- To delight yourself in the *Lord* first! Because when we do, his desires become our desires (by our choosing) and he will give us the desires of our heart (Psalm 37:4).

Discontentment Stunts our Spiritual Growth

The discontented person looks around and says, "I deserve something better than this." Because he is never happy and never satisfied, he drags others into the swamp with him. No wonder

---

[21] Cheyenne Olson, My 15 Minutes: Genesis 3:1, The Seeds of Discontentment
[22] Ibid

Benjamin Franklin declared, "Contentment makes a poor man rich; discontentment makes a rich man poor." Discontentment is the cancer of the soul. It eats away our joy, corrodes our happiness, destroys our outlook on life, and produces a terminal jaundice of the soul so that everything looks negative to us.

The Israelites, according to Scripture, continuously complained and failed to be directed by the sovereign hand of God. The Israelites provide illustration after illustration pertaining to the challenged with discontentment. As they journeyed out of Egypt toward Canaan, their complaining is documented for an example. No one was affected as much as was Moses, who often was frustrated, deregulated, even angry because of the blatant discontentment, which would precipitate God's judgment.

The deliverance of Israel was ocular demonstration of God's providence as these slaves to Pharaoh would be released from captivity to journey to Canaan but would not see the land because of their rebellion. God would show his power in their release as he brought Pharaoh's reign of the people to an abrupt end.

The Israelites were privy to the unlimited power of God as his judgment and of his mercy was seen in Exodus 14:31. God should well be honored over Pharaoh and the Egyptians as witnessed by Israel. After this overthrow of their king and his host, the Egyptians interrupted them no more in their journey and were convinced of the omnipotence of Israel's protector. Israel, with such displays of the justice and mercy, should never have been deficient in faith, neither should they have complained or murmured.

The Israelites rejoiced in Exodus 15:1–22; however, this elation was short lived and their view changed quickly as the Bible says, "And the people murmured against Moses, saying, 'What shall we drink'" (Exod. 15:24).

What can believers today learn from the discontented behavior of the Israelites?

THE QUEST FOR CONTENTMENT

Discontentment Manifests When We Focus on What We Don't Have

William B. Barclay stated, *"Those who grumble against the Lord are guilty of rebellion against him."*[23] After all that the Israelites witnessed, they should have given great praise that God would not leave or forsake them. The solution was so simple. The Lord had no intention of abandoning his people. He just wanted their trust (Prov. 3:5–6).

Discontentment Exhibits Dissatisfaction with God

Why didn't the Israelites take inventory of how God had provided for them (Ex. 14:31, 15:1–21, 16:4–5, 17:6)? Have you taken inventory of the times that you've complained? I'm sure it was a pretty picture. Contentment requires faith in God. Vickie Kraft in an article said, *"They should have encouraged one another about God's daily provision while in the wilderness, but they didn't."*[24]

Discontentment Is a Mistrusting of God

Contentment is trusting God implicitly. Thus, discontent is the opposite of faith. When we worry about our needs, as did Israel, we are telling God that we don't trust him to provide for us. We may not say it with words, but our actions tell him this. God knows our heart. He understands why we worry, but it's simply a lack of trust in God's promise that he will provide for our every need if only we seek him first (Matthew 6:33). Jesus asked, *"Which of you by being anxious can add a single hour to his span of life"* (Matthew 6:27)? In fact, worry can only shorten our life span; so let's dump the worry and put our trust in God.

Discontentment Amounts to Complaining against God's Plan

The people of Israel, although God met their every need, were dissatisfied with the plan and purpose of God. Believers today are no different as God continues to supply our needs daily (Phil. 4:19). The believer's heart must not yearn for the world but sacrificing

---

[23] William B. Barclay, *The Secret of Contentment* (P & R Publishing, 2010). p. 54
[24] Vickie Kraft, *Facing Your Feelings*, February 7, 2007

our bodies to God (Rom. 12:1–2). Israel yearned for Egypt and the lifestyle of their hearts were accustomed to, as they were slaves to their cravings. They had selective memory as they blanked out the agony of slavery. Their constant dissatisfaction and complaining led to rebellion. This time God was finished with them but God reached his limit of longsuffering with Israel as he informed them that no one who has treated me with contempt will ever see Canaan (Num. 14:20–23).

Discontentment Manifests Itself in Sin

The temptation to sin usually begins with discontentment about what we are or what we have. Israel had everything needed but discontentment via complaining reared its ugly head because of ungodly thoughts and attitudes. Their ungrateful, discontented spirit opened the door to unholy behavior, causing them to turn their backs on God and take matters into their own hands. This kind of rebellion doesn't have to happen. God is faithful, and we don't have to yield to the temptation to be discontented with our families, salaries, jobs, and life in general. Temptation doesn't have to lead to sin but yielding to it will.

6

Conquering Materialism

*Be content with what you have;
rejoice in the way things are. When you realize there is
nothing lacking, the whole world belongs to you.*
—Jeremiah Burroughs

Materialism has forced people to think about their material needs even above God. In this chapter we will explore, identify, and focus on how we can prevail against the materialistic world perspective of our day. I realize that contentment is an active and dynamic process; however, it doesn't have to be a struggle between what you need as opposed to desire.

Dr. Ryan T. Howell, an Associate Professor of Psychology at San Francisco State University, says,

> *The belief that material possessions improve individuals' personal and social well-being permeates America. However, contrary to this belief, multiple studies show that materialists, compared to non-materialists, have lower social and personal well-being. Compulsive and impulsive spending, increased debt, decreased savings, depression, social anxiety, decreased subjective well-being, less psychological satisfaction, and other undesirable outcomes have*

all been linked with materialistic values and purchasing behaviors."[25]

Many people today believe that contentment is getting what we desire but this mindset is contrary to biblical precepts. Contentment is quietly resting in God's providence, *"But my God shall supply all your need according to his riches in glory by Christ Jesus" (Phil. 4:19)*

The impact of materialism in society is a complex subject. Materialism can be defined as a dominating sense of desire to pursue wealth and other tangible things that can provide physical comforts that ignore the importance of spiritual values. Some characteristics of materialistic people are non-generosity, envy, and possessiveness to name a few. Their hunger for money, proclivity to get rich and love of money are antecedents of discontentment but if we trust God, we will want for nothing and will be fully contented with God's favor and blessing (Prov. 19:23).

Captured by Materialism
Botox, nose jobs, lip jobs, breast augmentations, liposuction, butt lifts, tummy tucks, and hair transplants. Look at how insidious advertising has captured and duped the world, Christians as well, into a false sense of happiness. It doesn't matter whether it's television, radio, or newspaper. Dr. Art Markman communicates, *"We live in a world of advertising."*[26]

Advertising affects us in many areas of life. The effects can be seen physically, emotionally, and relationally. Advertising has become so prevalent it tells us what type of car to buy, what kind of toothpaste to use, even the brand of clothing we should wear.

---

[25] Dr. Ryan T. Howell, What Causes Materialism in America? Psychology Today, March 23, 2014
[26] Art Markman, What Does Advertising Do? Psychology Today, August 31, 2010

According to the ASPS annual plastic surgery statistics report, there were more than 17.7 million surgical and minimally invasive cosmetic procedures performed in the United States in 2018. More than 1.8 million cosmetic surgical procedures performed in 2018, the top five were:[27]

1. *Breast augmentation (313,735 procedures, up four percent from 2017)*
2. *Liposuction (258,558 procedures, up five percent from 2017)*
3. *Nose reshaping (213,780 procedures, down two percent from 2017)*
4. *Eyelid surgery (206,529 procedures, down one percent from 2017)*
5. *Tummy tuck (130,081 procedures, about the same as 2017)*

Materialism is at the forefront of much debt today. Consider credit card debt and how this country alone is being ravaged by debt. So many people can't seem to get out of their own way in terms of overspending to assuage their desire to fit in, be recognized, or stand out amongst their peers.

The credit card industry has a huge effect on everyday life in the US. The average American owns multiple credit cards with balances reaching thousands of dollars. It is the tragedy of our times and the epidemic of not being content that has plunged us into a material abyss. It doesn't matter how much money we earn, or how many blessings come our way, more is never enough.

Consider the latest Credit Card Usage and Ownership Statistics (2019 Report):[28]

How many credit cards does the average person have?   *3.1*
What is the average credit card debt per person?   *$6,354*

---

[27] American Society of Plastic Surgeons, New Plastic Surgery Statistics Reveal Trends Toward Body Enhancement, March 11, 2019
[28] Value Penguin, Credit Card Usage and Ownership Statistics (2019 Report)

What is the average credit score?	*675*
What is the average credit utilization rate?	*30%*
How many credit cards are there in the U.S.?	*1.5 billion*
How much credit card debt is there in the U.S.?	*$815 billion*
What percentage of people have a credit card?	*67%*

Our society teaches us that chasing contentment is found in the smartest phone, the lightest laptop, the latest flat screen television, the biggest wedding, the most luxurious home, the tightest figure. Contentment is not about the "just as soon as mentality." Just as soon as I get the latest pair of Jordan's (for young people reading this book). Just as soon as I make enough money, I'll settle down and have a family. Just as soon as I get through the tough time I'm going through, I'll eat better.

How do you avoid the trap of materialism and live a life of contentment? We must realize, as did Paul that passing through many conditions will prepare and settle the believer for contentment. The endless cycle of materialism will never teach contentment. God desires for his children to bear abundance with meekness, and hard times with contentment, "I know both how to be abased, and I know how to abound: everywhere and in all things I am instructed both to be full and to be hungry, both to abound and suffer need" (Phil. 4:12).

The Benchmark
Merriam-Webster defines benchmark *as "something that serves as a standard by which others may be measured or judged."*[29] The Bible is God's benchmark for truth in a deceived world, "Sanctify them through thy truth: thy word is truth" (John 17:17). Are we prepared to use this benchmark as our standard? There's no question that materialism is sinful and not of God.

---

[29] Merriam-Webster Dictionary

Rob Hoveman, in his article entitled "Marxism and the Meaning of Materialism," says,

> *Materialism for many people means two things: firstly, an obsession with material things (possessions, conspicuous wealth and consumption), and secondly, a rejection of theism (a belief in God and spirit) and acceptance of the view that the natural world of which we are part is all there is.*[30]

Materialism must never become the benchmark for a believer, neither should it keep us from the sweet virtue of contentment. Too many believers are in pursuit of material possessions, which have caused them to falter, fall short of, and even desert the faith. Let us do as Paul instructed about using the Word as a benchmark, *"Examine yourselves, whether ye be in the faith; prove your own selves. Know ye not your own selves, how that Jesus Christ is in you, except ye be reprobates"* (2 Cor. 13:5).

Adverse Results of Materialism

What does materialism promote? The byproducts of materialism are lust, envy, false comfort, and idolatry. Materialism is diametrically opposed to selflessness, and compassion. Materialism promotes a lack of morals. Materialistic people thrive doing what they believe is right, are focused on riches (often by any means necessary), and lack morality. Materialistic people, at their core, are dominated by sin.

The above results of materialism is sin and its consequences are destructive. The Bible tells us that God has created man with an ability to make decision and choices. The question is what the decision and choices will lead to in terms of God's righteousness (Rom. 6:23) and the wages of sin (Rom. 3:23).

---

[30] Rob Hoveman, Marxism and the Meaning of Materialism, Socialistworker.org, February 12, 2018

Money isn't just something to help buy necessities and live a comfortable life for those who are materialistic. People driven by money have ambitions to live lavishly, often beyond their means, and this leads to sin. Believers who commit this sin will find themselves distanced from God. Here are some ways a believer's faith is impacted by materialism:

1. *Deficient of Contentment*

The problem with believers who are discontent begins with the heart. Our heart contains thoughts, emotions, desires, feelings, beliefs. The heart is where we become discontent with things in life regardless if they are good or bad. The heart is the seat of complaining, thus our hearts must learn to be content, "All the days of the afflicted are evil: but he that is of a merry heart hath a continual feast" (Prov. 15:15). The state of the heart governs the outward condition, my friends. Are you satisfied with all the allotments of God's providence?

2. *Consistent Longing*

When a person is not contented and satisfied, there will be consistent and persistent longing for what they don't have despite what God has provided. When is enough simply enough? Will anything ever be enough for the materialistic person?
What are you longing for currently in your life? Allow Christ to be your source of joy. Allow what Christ wants to be what you want. Let love and gratitude transform your desire so that what you long for pleases him (Psa. 37:4)

3. *Emotional Distress*

Now when a person is enveloped by materialism, there's nothing that will make him feel happy and that's simply because he isn't contented with anything. The materialist continues to seek the house in Aspen, to have more money than Bill Gates, and to live extravagantly. Robert A. Johnson said it best, "Contentment is not the result of what you have or what you do in life."[31]

Both our bodily and spiritual interests will be safe when we place them in the Lord's hands, and, through the peace which will result from our faith, our thoughts will become steady, calm, resolute, and joyful (Prov. 16:3).

If you find yourself enveloped by materialism, pray and seek God for help (1 Pet. 5:7). It will be very hard to change your heart on your own. Truth is, materialism is like an addiction, but the good news is God is greater than any addiction (Psa. 20:1).

---

[31] Robert A. Johnson and Jerry M. Ruhl, Contentment: A Way to True Happiness, (Harper One), 3

7

Money, Money, Money

He is rich or poor according to what he is,
not according to what he has.
—Henry Ward Beecher

As we continue to learn the importance of contentment, a key area must be addressed, that being money. The O'Jays, in 1973, sang a song entitled "For The Love of Money." The impetus of the song is a direct reflection of how money, when loved, leads man into spiritual ruin.

Scripture gives us direct insight into how the love of money is diametrically opposed to contentment:

> But godliness with contentment is great gain. For we brought nothing into this world, and it is certain we can carry nothing out. And having food and raiment let us be therewith content. But they that will be rich fall into temptation and a snare, and into many foolish and hurtful lusts, which drown men in destruction and perdition. For the love of money is the root of all evil: which while some coveted after, they have erred from the faith, and pierced themselves through with many sorrows. (1 Timothy 6:6–10)

The Word of God provides a lens through which we should be looking at money and the material things of this life. I'm thankful that in his Word he put in the appropriate verses to help show us the biblical concept of money and how to appropriately use money.

Money, power, and material wealth have ruined many lives, not only in our country, but throughout the rest of the world as well. The Bible tells us that it is not the money itself that will corrupt and ruin a person and his life; rather it is the love of and abnormal pursuit of that money that will ruin a person and his life.

Learning contentment for the believer should include an emphasis on how to treat wealth differently than non-believers. Believers, because of their spiritual nature, should think about money differently, use it differently, and ultimately, be content regardless of their life condition (Phil. 4:11).

There's no doubt how difficult it is to fully comprehend the concept of contentment as it relates to money. We know very well the seductive attraction of wealth. Are you free from the love of money? Has money driven you to say and do things that violate the character of God? Learning contentment doesn't happen overnight, yet it is a process fueled by faith and discipline which originates from the heart and is commanded by God (Prov. 4:23; Heb. 13:5).

Great Gain

Paul indicates that we are to walk in *"godliness,"* along with being content (1 Tim. 6:6). Godliness is holy living. God reminds us that we must not only submit to his commands but seek to imitate his holiness, "But as he which hath called you is holy, so be ye holy in all manner of conversation; Because it is written, Be ye holy; for I am holy" (1 Pet. 1:15–16).

Paul is communicating that it is great gain to be content with whatever we have, whatever we may receive, and in whatever condition we find ourselves in. Learning to be godly is significant in that sanctification is a process that transforms us into the image of his Son.

This verse is instructing us to pursue godliness, which exemplifies a demeanor that Christians should cultivate, then exhibit. 1 Timothy 6:6 ushers us to the reality that "godliness," is deeply committed spirituality. *"Contentment is the Christians readiness to be satisfied with God meeting our basic needs, without yearning for unnecessary luxuries"*[32] It is clear that contentment derives from being cognizant of and trust in God, *"Not that we are sufficient of ourselves to think anything as of ourselves; but our sufficiency is of God" (2 Cor. 3:5).*

Exit Strategy

1 Timothy 6:7 offers the Christian a perspective that puts his view of money in perspective. Man enters this life with nothing, he will depart this life with nothing. When we juxtapose our entering with departing, there's no doubt it is a divine means of showing man that since material wealth is relatively insignificant, he should pursue the important things, *"But thou, O man of God, flee these things; and follow after righteousness, godliness, faith, love, patience, meekness" (1 Tim. 6:11).*

Please know that in no way am I against money, wealth, and material possessions; however, we must remember we came into this world naked, without any worldly provisions (Job 1:21; Psa. 49:17). The Bible reminds us that riches are transitory (Prov. 27:24).

Forget not that we are tenants traveling through this land, hoping to reach our destination, that being heaven. The Christian should exhibit hearts that love heaven's treasures, *"Lay not up for ourselves treasures upon earth, where moth and rust doth corrupt, and where thieves break through and steal: But lay up for yourselves treasures in heaven, where neither moth nor rust doth corrupt, and where thieves do not break through nor steal: For where your treasure is, there will your heart be also" (Matt. 6:19–21).*

---

[32] Jerome D. Quinn and William C. Wacker, *The First and Second Letters to Timothy* (ECC, Grand Rapids: Earmands, 2000), p. 218

The Christian should give thanks in advance for God who sent his Son ahead to prepare our destination (Jn. 14:1–4). I'm grateful and excited about heaven, knowing there's nothing here on earth that I need to bring with me. No person, place, or thing can substitute what God has awaiting me. What awaits the Christian? *"To an inheritance incorruptible, and undefiled, and that fadeth not away, reserved in heaven for you" (1 Pet. 1:4).*

Ultimately, we should be content because we haven't brought anything into this world. We should have no gain-seeking anxiety because it is the breeder of discontent (Matt. 6:25).

All I Need
If God provides you with all you need or more than is necessary for you, take it thankfully (1 Thess. 5:18) and use it for God's glory. On the other hand, if God provides no more than is necessary for you, will you complain? Let us be content!

In 1 Timothy 6:8, the verse takes us deeper into the quest for contentment communicating that the necessities of life bring contentment, not money, wealth, and material possessions. I'm convinced that Matthew 6:33 helps provide great clarity for finding contentment with the basic necessities of life, *"But seek ye first the kingdom of God, and his righteousness; and all these things shall be added unto you."*

Have you completely surrendered your life to Christ? Have you expressed, Lord, I want your will more than my own to be done? Have you accepted the truth that all you need is available to you and God wants to provide it? Are you seeking God's rule and reign?

Avoid the Fall
It has been said that money is like a fresh bag of potato chips: half substance and half air. We purchase those chips hoping that when we open the bag it will be completely full. Why do we continue in this futile pursuit hoping it will bring satisfaction? It is the same

for our desire to have money. Money is necessary. We need it for food and shelter. That is the substance part. The rest of it is simply vapor.

In 1 Timothy 6:9, Timothy is instructed to avoid covetousness because of its outcome. Timothy is further instructed to enforce the duty of contentment because of the evil that rears its ugly head as result of the quest to be rich. When man takes his focus off God, then wickedness, sensual pleasures, and lust follow. *"A faithful man shall abound with blessings: but he that maketh haste to be rich shall not be innocent" (Prov. 28:20).*

What then remains but destruction for the body and perdition for the soul? The Christian should drive hard toward contentment, keeping himself from plunging into an irrecoverable abyss of ruin and destruction. What's more valuable—your soul or the worldly possessions that you will ultimately lose (Mark 8:36)?

Some would say that Satan's greatest resource in his effort to take our focus off God is money. Money is universal. It affects all of us. We need to remember how easily money can be a stumbling block whenever we are tempted to give our love and sense of security to our bank accounts.

The Power of Money

Timothy concludes on how money is not evil but the love of it is disastrous, "For the love of money is the root of all evil: which while some coveted after, they have erred from the faith, and pierced themselves through with many sorrows" (1 Timothy 6:10).

This verse is often misquoted as saying, *"Money is the root of all evil."* Notice how "money" is substituted for *"love of money"* and *"the root of all evil"* is substituted for *"a root of all kinds of evil."* These changes, while subtle, have an enormous impact on the meaning of the verse.

Timothy is redirected from the snare of the enemy. Timothy is instructed that the real source of *"great gain"* is godliness with true contentment (v. 6). Contentment, in a biblical sense, is the recognition that we come into the world with nothing and that everything we have is a gift from God's hands (verses 7–8). When one desires to be rich (loving money); temptation is present, and a fall is inevitable (v. 9). A misinterpretation of God's Word, abandonment of his precepts, and wandering from the faith leads to trouble and disquiet (Prov. 1:20–33).

8

Cultivating Contentment

We have to cultivate contentment with what we have. We really don't need much. When you know this, the mind settles down. Cultivate generosity. Delight in giving. Learn to live lightly. In this way, we can begin to transform what is negative into what is positive. This is how we start to grow up.
—*Tenzin Palmo*

We have traveled a great distance in our quest to discover, learn, and apply contentment to our everyday lives. Cultivating contentment is another ingredient we must discuss. Contentment, after it is learned, must be cultivated, which promotes the idea of working to make it better.

The World Can't Provide True Fulfillment
The beginning of cultivating contentment is accepting the fact that nothing here can make us permanently happy, by showing how empty all things are, how short a time man has to possess them; and that, while this time lasts, he can only enjoy the same empty things over and over again, till he be discontent with them, *"Vanity of vanities, saith the Preacher, vanity of vanities; all is vanity" (Eccl. 1:2)*.

We live in a world that delights in wealth, status, material possessions, and other temporary things of this world, but are never satisfied. It should be stated that we never truly get what we want, which is why we are always left wanting more. Man's cupidity is as insatiable as the grave, *"Hell and destruction are never full; so the eyes of man are never satisfied"* (Prov. 27:20).

What we often fail to accept is that all created good void of God is unsuitable and insufficient to make us happy, or to do anything effectual toward it. Every enjoyment is unsatisfactory without God. The perceived happiness and/or satisfaction of man is uncertain, and transient, and there is nothing permanent or stable to be found.

There's a story about a man who believed he had a good life and felt lucky for all the things he had. He was married to a loving wife, had a good job, owned a nice house, and had three healthy kids, yet he felt incomplete, unhappy, and communicated something was missing in his life. To pursue anything but God is a fast track to frustrated inadequacy. Earthly pursuits are the occasions of innumerable cares, and fears, and sorrows, and mischiefs.

Hilary Jacobs Hendel tells the story of Mike, who, in spite of his good fortune, could not shake the nagging feeling that he wasn't enough. "I should be more successful. I should make more money. I should be where my boss is. I should have a graduate degree. I should have a bigger house. I should have more friends."[33] What plagues you today? Are you seeking contentment outside of God's providential care?

There is nothing on earth that can make us permanently happy. God shows man how empty all things are, how short a time man has to possess things, and that, while this time lasts, he can only enjoy the same empty things over and over again, till he be discontent with them.

Man can't love God and love the world for they are incompatible. God calls for his children to make a choice. What is your

---

[33] Hilary Jacobs Hendel, Psychology Today, *Why Do I Feel So Inadequate? An Approach to Healing.* May 20, 2018

choice today? Who have you decided to follow? Our relationship with God must not be an appendix to our busy, worldly lives. The believer must be set apart from the world. Believers are in the world physically but not of it, neither should they be part of its values, *"I have given them thy word: and the world hath hated them, because they are not of the world, even as I am not of the world. I pray not that thou shouldest take them out of the world, but that thou shouldest keep them from the evil" (Jn. 17:14–15).*

God's Best for Us Cultivates Contentment

Will you as a believer ever be deeply fulfilled, joyful, or truly "happy" with the things this world has to offer? Is God your joy, peace, and hope? It is essential, as believers, that God has first place in our lives. Let me pause to remind you that God's provisions for us will never be less than what the world offers to us, *"Every good gift and every perfect gift is from above, and cometh down from the Father of lights, with whom is no variableness, neither shadow of turning" (Jas. 1:17).*

Again, I'm not opposed to believers being blessed (Eccl. 5:18–20); however, if we truly place our priority on the Lord, chances are, our heart's greatest desires will not be possessions, status, or wealth, but rather the eternal treasures we find in following Christ.

This world can never satisfy our deepest longings, but if we choose to delight in God's way, he will always provide above and beyond our expectations. Rhonda Stoppe says, *"True delight in Him causes us to take our sights off of what we want in order to long for what he desires."*[34] The more we come to know God through studying his Word, the more we will trust him to supply our needs and find contentment in his goodness. God has informed us, *"But my God shall supply all your need according to his riches in glory by Christ Jesus" (Phil. 4:19).*

---

[34] Rhonda Stoppe, *What Does it Mean to Delight Yourself in the Lord?* (Psalm 37:4), July 14, 2019

Deterrents to Cultivating Contentment

What drives man away from cultivating contentment? John paints a kaleidoscopic picture for us:

> Love not the world, neither the things that are in the world. If any man love the world, the love of the Father is not in him. For all that is in the world, the lust of the flesh, and the lust of the eyes, and the pride of life, is not of the Father, but is of the world. And the world passeth away, and the lust thereof: but he that doeth the will of God abideth for ever. (1 Jn. 2:15–17)

This battle to cultivate contentment, found in this text, provides working evidence as to why man is discontent and is hoodwinked into a consciousness overwhelmed by the lust of the flesh, lust of the eyes, and the pride of life.

As believers, we must steer clear of focusing on what the world flaunts before us but should embrace and be thankful for the sufficiency of God and him alone (this cultivates contentment). Man has fallen into the chasm of colorful decoys and shiny wrappers that have rendered him bankrupt as a God-created producer, *"And God blessed them, saying, 'Be fruitful, and multiply, and fill the waters in the seas, and let fowl multiply in the earth'" (Gen. 1:22)*.

The lust of the flesh, in simple terms, are the cravings of fallen nature that attempts to live independent of God. The desires of the flesh always give birth to the works of the flesh (Gal. 5:19–21). This is why man cannot realize his proclivity to produce, instead he seeks to consume because this is the bent of the world he has become comfortable living in.

The lust of the eyes, in simple terms, is the way we look at things or what we look at. This is what tripped up Adam and Eve in the garden (Gen. 3:6). *Eve became the first consumer!* Contentment is a by-product of being a producer (God created us to produce—Gen. 1:22). Contentment is inward and spiritual. When cultivating contentment, it relies on the satisfaction we have because of God's sufficiency. This means the lenses we look through either moves us toward contentment and the consciousness of becoming and remaining a producer or one who daily chases people, places, and things that will never fully satisfy.

The pride of life (possessions), in simple terms, is pride in what you believe you possess. A believer cultivating contentment is an individual who can sit quietly under the reassuring reality that God is all they need, that again his sufficiency is enough. A believer who seeks God daily doesn't need to seek affirmation, validation, or accolades from the world. Believers cultivating contentment are driven by the truth that God alone is enough, and we are his children (Col. 1:15–17).

I assert that our ability to cultivate contentment recognizes, understands and makes practical application of 1 John 2:15–17. When we adhere to the principles of God's Word, putting into practice being content, then we know our love for God is on a solid foundation.

9

Characteristics of Contentment

How does a Christian ascertain if they're attaining a passing grade in the school of contentment? How is a student recognized to be making progress in this quest for contentment? Jeremiah Burroughs declares, *"A contented heart looks to God's disposal, and submits to God's disposal, that is, he sees the wisdom of God in everything."*[35] When the believer begins to see contentment through the lens of God's providence, then he is learning true contentment.

The school of contentment requires intestinal fortitude, inner focus, and a commitment to godliness. The book of Philippians was where we started and has been the central focus on this Quest for Contentment. It is relevant now to consider characteristics that empower the student to live out contentment.

The people of God, those of faith, can know that contentment has be attained as delineated by these biblical characteristics. These five are the works of Thomas Watson:[36]

---

[35] Jeremiah Burroughs, *The Rare Jewel of Christian Contentment* (Edinburgh: Banner of Truth, 1979) P. 13
[36] Thomas Watson, *The Art of Divine Contentment* (Free Presbyterian Publications), p. 95–99

A Contented Spirit Is a Silent Spirit

With reference to God, the one who is content is not complaining against God, he does not grumble and murmur... Remember well the distinction between complaining to God and complaining about God. When we complain to God, we are bringing our problems and vices and crying out to God for wisdom, grace, and help. When we are complaining about God we are attacking his character... Silence is a reflection of peaceful trust—even amid circumstances that are difficult to understand while anger, grumbling, and complaining represent inner turmoil and a lack of trust in God.

A Contented Spirit Is a Cheerful Spirit

Contentment is more than patience (though it is not less). It involves a cheerfulness of the soul... Could you be accused of being cheerful, even amid difficulty?

A Contented Spirit Is a Thankful Spirit

Anyone can thank God for prosperity but the contented person blesses him when afflicted (2 Cor. 6:10; Phil. 4:9–11). The discontented heart is ever complaining of their condition, but the contented spirit is always thanking God for it.

A Contented Spirit Is Not Bound by Circumstances

Because contentment works from the inside out, it is shielded from the ever changing circumstances outside of us. Remember Paul himself said that his contentment was seen "in any and every circumstance" (Phil. 4:12).

A Contented Spirit Will Not Avoid Trouble by Means of Sin

Resting in God's providence does not mean that we stand still. Contentment does not mean complacency. However, when we have something we want to pursue, but God has not made it available, a contented spirit does not rush ahead anyway. A discontented spirit will not wait. If God does not open the door of his providence, "they will break it open and wind themselves out of affliction by sin; bringing their souls into trouble; this is far from holy contentment, this is unbelief broken into rebellion." Contentment would rather wait upon God than sin against God.

Precepts to Remember

I believe that contentment can be seen in a believer when the following biblical precepts are manifested:

1. *Remember the earth is the Lord's* (Psa. 24:1).

This passage expresses the supreme and infinite dominion of God over all creation. Contentment begins with acknowledging who creates, governs, and preserves.

2. *Remember God's promises* (2 Cor. 1:20).

All of God's promises are ratified through his Word. Believers should be content knowing that God doesn't use worldly, sinful men as instruments of his glory but those who are bound by godliness. Therefore, Paul felt himself bound to maintain a character of the strictest veracity. The believer can rest because of the promises that God made to man through his Son Jesus Christ. God fully and immutably performs his promises, in this truth I can be content.

3. *Remember to put to death your sinful nature* (Col. 3:5b).

God commands that the worldly desires in man die, that his spiritual desires live. Contentment drives out the vices that are natural to the old man (Rom. 6:6), empowering the righteousness of God (Rom. 1:17) to become evident. The heart of the contented is diametrically opposed to Satan's modus operandi. The contented subdues their debasing passions so that holiness guides their lives (Rom.12:1–2).

4. *Remember to guard your heart* (Matt. 6:19–21).

Man must never be content with the things of this world. God requires the whole heart of man and it's unthinkable to believe him to share (Exod. 34:14–16). God is jealous for us because he fiercely loves us and will accept nothing less than commitment. God abhors those who attempt to worship anything except himself. Man makes competitors and corrivals when he subjects himself to the solicitation of worldly possessions. God wants man to rush headlong into the unmerited bounty he freely provides. What is the condition of your heart (Deut. 10:16)?

5. *Remember not to envy others* (Jam. 3:14–16).

I will not linger long here because nothing presents us more unfit than envy and strife. Christian zeal has a proclivity toward love. God is not the author of earthly, sensual, and devilish behavior. Wisdom from above is void of demonic influence and those who learn contentment have quiet spirits which long for love, *"Love looks through a telescope; envy a microscope" (Josh Billings).*

6. *Remember to keep a disdain for greed* (Lk. 12:15).

Does your life thrive on what it possesses or seeks to possess? God is the believer's source, sustenance, and supplier. The abundance of our possessions will never be enough to bring contentment. Such a disposition of mind is never satisfied; for, as soon as one object is gained, the heart goes out after another. Earthly riches will never procure contentment. Is your life expressed in the earthly things you have or what you are?

7. *Remember to live in humility* (Jam. 4:6).

Humility is one of the toughest qualities to develop and consistently live out for the believer; because the very nature of humility appears to be counterintuitive to the view of the world.

Independence, prestige, success is all applauded by the world. There can be no divine contentment without humility. The spirit of God produces both. The humble man is contented with God. Let us bow prostrate adoring, exalting, magnifying God.

8. *Remember to focus on blessing others* (2 Cor. 9:5–8).

Dallas Willard says,

> Blessing is the projection of good into the life of another. It isn't just words. It's the actual putting forth of your will for the good of another person. It always involves God, because when you will the good of another person, you realize only God is capable of bringing that.[37]

Contentment is being steeped in God's grace. God's grace moves the believer to give to another that which he has received. When you focus on blessing others, God always ensures you are abundantly blessed.

---

[37] Dallas Willard, *The Right Way to Give Someone a Blessing*, Christianity Today, January 8, 2014

Conclusion

This Quest for Contentment was born out of my own discontent and desire to learn as did Paul (Phil. 4:11). I then moved with intent to biblically define contentment, how to pursue and attain it, and finally sustain it. It has been a work to identify, understand, and live a life of contentment.

The great Puritan writer, Jeremiah Burroughs, said, *"Contentment is to be learned as a great mystery, and those who are thoroughly trained in this art, which like Samson's riddle to a natural man, have learned a deep mystery."*[38]

I trust that you will, in your daily walk with the Lord, "learn" as did Paul the art of contentment so you can, with his strength, make practical application of the words written in this book, especially in the Word of God.

More importantly, I hope that prayer will pilot you through the ups and downs, changes, and turnarounds of life as you journey on your quest for contentment. Thomas Watson, another great Puritan, said, *"The last rule for contentment is, be much in prayer. Beg of God, that he will work our hearts to this blessed frame."*[39]

I often wondered what drove people like Mother Theresa, Martin Luther King, and Mahatma Gandhi to commit their lives for the cause of others. I conclude that at the core of their work were lives that learned how to be "content" (Philippians 4:10–19).

---

[38] Jeremiah Burroughs, *The Rare Jewel of Christian Contentment* (Edinburgh: Banner of Truth, 1979) p. 1

[39] Thomas Watson, *The Art of Divine Contentment* (Free Presbyterian Publications), p. 114

About the Author

Martin Freeman (B.A, Th.M., Th.D., LSW) has extensive leadership experience. He has been bi-vocational throughout his time in ministry. He has been a church planter and senior pastor. Martin currently serves as a Student Advocate Specialist Supervisor/McKinney Vento Liaison—Youngstown City School District. Martin enjoys teaching, family, children, and is an avid golfer.

CPSIA information can be obtained
at www.ICGtesting.com
Printed in the USA
BVHW092305051022
648789BV00002B/106